Tecumseh

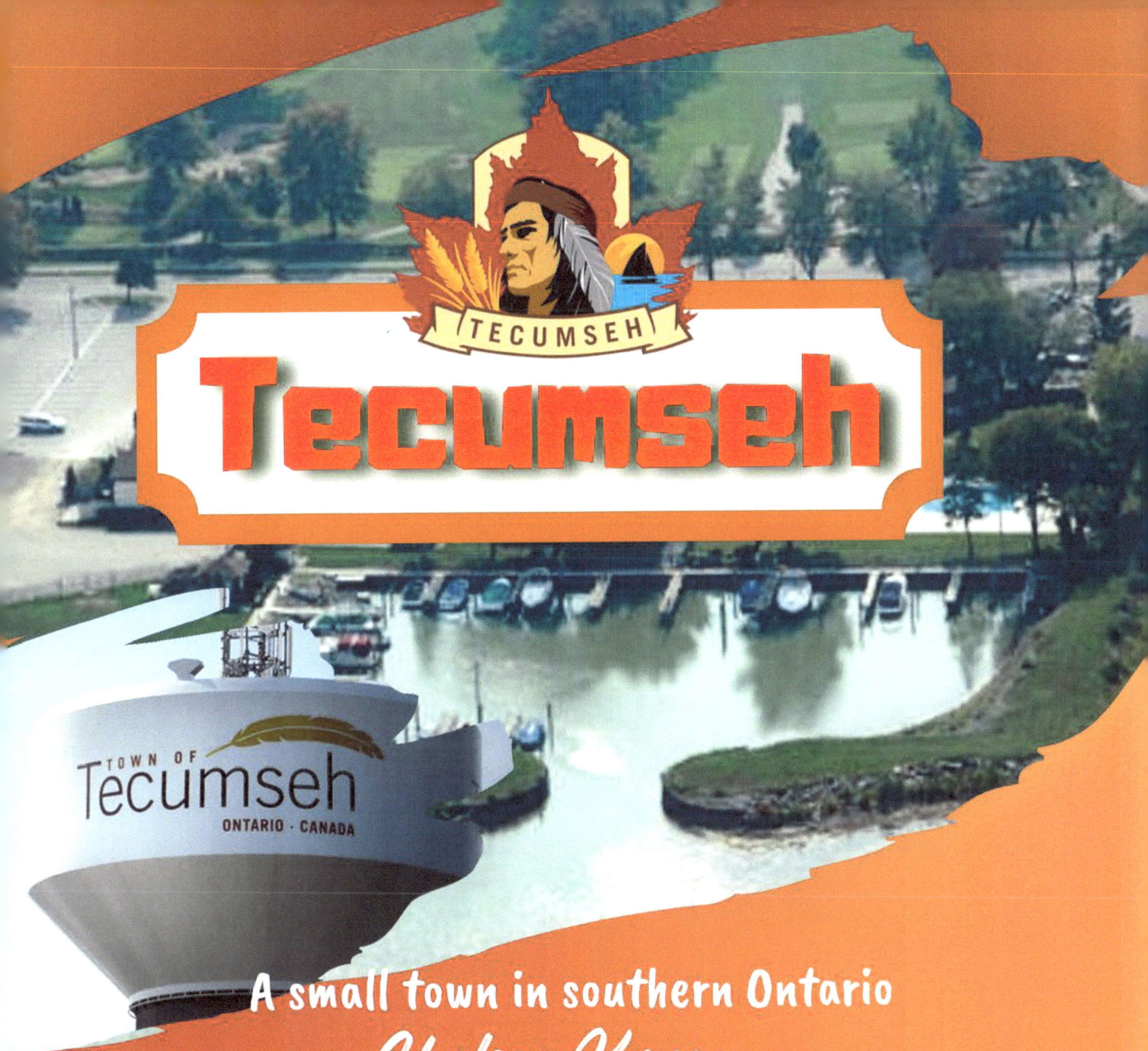

A small town in southern Ontario

Chelsea Kong

PRINTED IN 2024-2025, MADE IN TORONTO, CANADA
ISBN: 978-1-998335-32-9
HARDCOVER ISBN: 978-1-998335-33-6
LIBRARY AND ARCHIVES CANADA

Tecumseh is a small town in South
Ontario found beside Windsor.
It is part of Windsor-Essex Country.

It's the town beside the City of Windsor.
There are 37 parks in this town.

The town is named as Chief Tecumseh.
He is a leader of the First Nations confederacy.
He was also a leader in the War of 1812.

Tecumseh was born in south-central Ohio in 1768. He moved to Ontario and died on October 5, 1813. He was near Thamesville, Ontario, when he died.

He fought in the war between Britain and the United States.

Tecumseh was an ally with the British.

He died in the Battle of Thames.

After he died, the Indigenous people kept fighting to keep their land and rights. This is the land that is called Tecumseh.

You will find Tecumseh's Town Hall.
Green Giant used to have a factory here.
The water tower is now used to say Tecumseh.

Tecumseh has 5 community parks.

Weston Park

Buster Reaume Park

Tecumseh Town Centre Park

Tecumseh Soccer Fields

St. Mary's Park

There are two Pickleball courts.
The main court has 10 courts.
Famous athletes compete there.

Zekelman Pickleball Complex

Shawanoe Park

Court Hours:

8:30 AM - 8:30 PM (Mon-Fri)

9:00 AM - 8:30 PM (Sat & Sun)

You can join the Pickleball Association. There is a Tecumseh Pickleball International Tournament every year. Windsor has several courts.

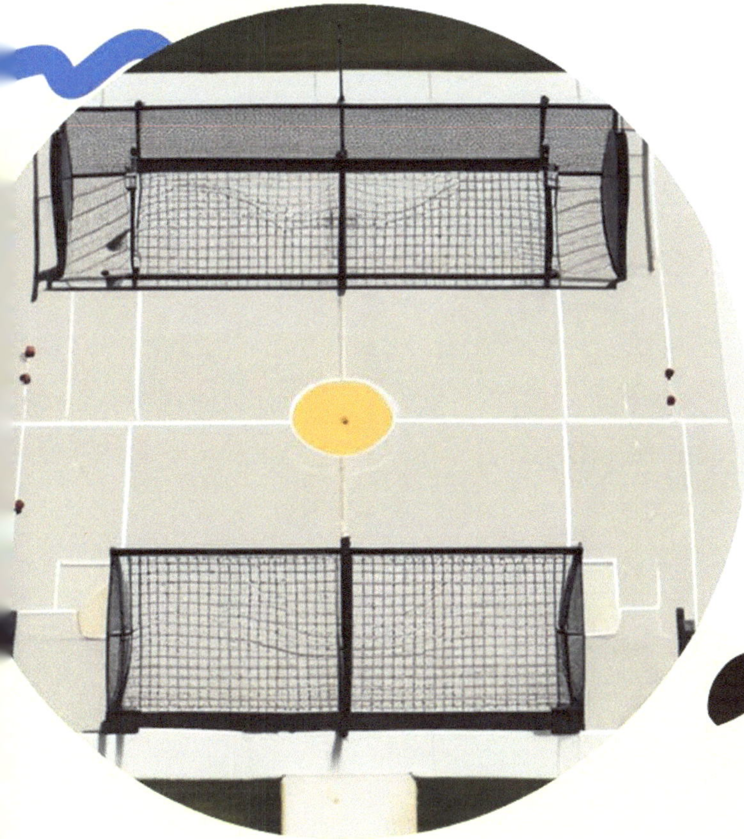

There are other sports played here.
They turned the Zekelman tennis courts
into a pickleball courts.

Tecumseh has 3 regional parks Lakewood Park, McAuliffe Park, and Lacasse Park

Tecumseh also has Lakewood Park and part of the Ganatchio Trail. The trail starts in Windsor.

Town of Tecumseh
Lakewood park

A.V. Graham Public School is one of the main schools for children.

St. Anne's Catholic High School used to be in Tecumseh, but moved to Belleville.

There are no colleges in Tecumseh.

Those who live in Tecumseh can go to

St. Clair College.

Tecumseh Public Library is CADA Library.

It was made better than before.

Transit

It has its on transit or transportation system called Tecumseh Transit Service (TTS).

It runs from Monday-Friday.

You can make ride requests for Saturday on Blaise Transit App.

Come visit Tecumseh Mall in Windsor.

It is the closest mall to Tecumseh.

References

THE CANADIAN ENCYCLOPIEDA, "TECUMSEH." THE CANADIAN ENCYCLOPEDIA. HTTPS://WWW.THECANADIANENCYCLOPEDIA.CA/EN/ARTICLE/TECUMSEH

"MEETING OF BROCK AND TECUMSEH, 1812 / RENCONTRE DE BROCK ET DU CHEF DE GUERRE TECUMSEH, 1812" BY BIBLIOARCHIVES / LIBRARYARCHIVES IS LICENSED UNDER CC BY 2.0.

Message from the Author

Thank you for reading this book. I hope you can leave a nice review to encourage me to write more books to teach children and adults. The Lord blesses you with all that you do. It will be nice to visit Tecumseh and enjoy this town. I like to travel there a few times in the year. I enjoy being in small towns rather than in a big city. People are friendly and enjoy their life. They learn to relax and are not in a hurry.

OTHER PRODUCTS

Knowing God
How to Hear God's Voice
New Life in Jesus
Loving Israel
God's Gifts/Spiritual Talents
Meeting God
Word Power
Fruit of the Spirit
The Tabernacle
Bride for Jesus
A Life of Prayer
Live Free
Who am I in Jesus
Walk in Love
God's Favor
Man of God
Woman of God
How to Use Money
God's Wisdom
Fasting
See Jerusalem and Bethany
First Fruit Offering
Feast of Trumpets
Day of Atonement
Feast of Tabernacles
Counting the Omer
Festival of Lights
Glory, Presence, and Holy Spirit
Live in God's Presence
Pentecost
See Galilee, Nazareth, and Tiberias
Hear God Speak
Knowing Jesus
Knowing Holy Spirit
A Healthy Life and Healthy Life Work Book
Smokey the Cat
Passover Unleavened Bread
Resurrection Life
The Blessing
Revival
Chelsea Learns Hebrew
Thanksgiving
Give Thanks
Jesus Birth
Loving Jesus: Bride and Groom
Proverbs 31 Woman

OTHER PRODUCTS

ABC of People in the Bible
Colours in the Bible
Breakthroughs
Open Doors
The Seven Spirits of God
Numbers in the Bible
Aglee the Eagle
An Eagle's Life
Chelsea Learns Numbers in Hebrew
ABC's of Faith
Feast of Purim
A Royal Life
Family Day
Family Blessings
Chinese New Year
Loving Jesus for Children
Worship
Pandas
Canada
Celia's Birthday
Animal Stories
Eagles
Fun in West Caribbean
Courtroom of of God
Fun in Yellowknife
Windsor

Coming soon

Fun in Labrador
Fun facts about Japan
Fragrances of Jesus

OTHER PRODUCTS

Devotionals

31 Day Devotional

Inspirational/Other

Chelsea's Psalms and Poems

Your Daily Meal: Chelsea's Photo Album

Chelsea's Psalms and Poems2

Travel West Caribbean

Chelsea's Recipes

Chelsea's Psalms and Poems3

Travel to Yellowknife

Puzzle Books

Biblical Puzzle Book Vol 1-5

Bible Puzzles for Young Children Book 1-3

Biblical Puzzle for Children Books 1-5

Chelsea's Bible Puzzles

Coming soon

Travel to Alberta

Travel to Labrador

Chelsea's Psalms and Poems 4

Travel Petra

OTHER PRODUCTS

Teaching Series

How to Hear God's Voice Teaching Guide & Audio Book

Relationship with God, Jesus, Holy Spirit Guide

Knowing God, Jesus, Holy Spirit Guide & Audio Book

Flowing in the Prophetic

Teaching (Non-Sale on my website)

Purim

Passover

Resurrection

B O O K R E V I E W S

More books on Amazon, Kobo, and Barnes and Noble, Smashwords, and IngramSpark.
https://chelseak532002550.wordpress.com/

More books on Amazon, Kobo, and Barnes and Noble, Smashwords, and IngramSpark.
https://www.amazon.com/author/chelseakong

Please leave a review and share with friends to help the author continue to write more books to reach more readers. Thank you so much for your support.

Review!

About CHELSEA KONG

She is a writer, creative arts and digital media artist, skilled administration and certified PCP (Payroll Compliance Professional), and podcaster. Chelsea also served in a variety of roles, from audiovisual, photography, to assisting on the worship team, and ministry team. She also has a passion for families being united.

Chelsea has been a guest on Unity Live Radio, The Lady Tracey Show, and How to Live for Christ and is highly recommended by a Proud Christian blog. She is also a guest blogger. A few of her books have been featured in YourAuthorHub, etc. She graduated from Hotel and Restaurant Management, Digital Media Arts, Office Administration, Payroll Compliance Professional, and experience working with children. Chelsea lives in Toronto, Canada. She mainly writes children's books, stories, bridal writing, poems, lyrics for songs, words of encouragement, blessings, prayers, and jokes. The author of How to Hear the Voice of God, the Bridal Collection, Knowing God, etc. She also has her own Bible Puzzle books and other inspired products. Her podcast channel is called Chelsea K on Anchor, Spotify, and iTunes.

Please check my website to find out more:
https://chelseak532002550.wordpress.com/

www.ingramcontent.com/pod-product-compliance
Ingram Content Group UK Ltd.
Pitfield, Milton Keynes, MK11 3LW, UK
UKHW061033310726
14089UKWH00010B/225
* 9 7 8 1 9 9 8 3 3 5 3 3 6 *